Steve Austin
The Story of the Wrestler They Call "Stone Cold"

Ric Flair
The Story of the Wrestler They Call "The Nature Boy"

Bill Goldberg

Bret Hart
The Story of the Wrestler They Call "The Hitman"

The Story of the Wrestler They Call "Hollywood" Hulk Hogan

Kevin Nash

Dallas Page
The Story of the Wrestler They Call "Diamond" Dallas Page

Pro Wrestling's Greatest Tag Teams

Pro Wrestling's Greatest Wars

Pro Wrestling's Most Punishing Finishing Moves

The Story of the Wrestler They Call "The Rock"

Randy Savage
The Story of the Wrestler They Call "Macho Man"

The Story of the Wrestler They Call "Sting"

The Story of the Wrestler They Call "The Undertaker"

Jesse Ventura
The Story of the Wrestler They Call "The Body"

The Women of Pro Wrestling

CHELSEA HOUSE PUBLISHERS

The Story of the Wrestler They Call "Diamond" Dallas Page

Jacqueline Mudge

Chelsea House Publishers
Philadelphia

Produced by Choptank Syndicate, Inc.

Editor and Picture Researcher: Mary Hull
Design and Production: Lisa Hochstein

CHELSEA HOUSE PUBLISHERS

Editor in Chief: Stephen Reginald
Production Manager: Pamela Loos
Art Director: Sara Davis
Director of Photography: Judy L. Hasday
Managing Editor: James D. Gallagher
Senior Production Editor: J. Christopher Higgins
Project Editor: Anne Hill
Cover Illustrator: Keith Trego

Cover Photos: Howard Kernats, Blackjack Brown

The Chelsea House World Wide Web site
address is http://www.chelseahouse.com

First Printing

1 3 5 7 9 8 6 4 2

Library of Congress Cataloging-in-Publication Data

Mudge, Jacqueline
    Diamond Dallas Page : the story of the wrestler they call "Diamond Dallas
Page" / by Jacqueline Mudge
        p. cm.— (Pro wrestling legends)
    Includes bibliographical references and index.
    Summary: A biography of the wrestler known as "Diamond" Dallas Page.
    ISBN 0-7910-5829-8 — ISBN 0-7910-5830-1 (pbk.)
    1. Diamond Dallas Page, 1949– —Juvenile literature. 2. Wrestlers—United
States—Biography—Juvenile Literature. [1. Diamond Dallas Page, 1949–
2. Wrestlers.] I. Title. II. Series.

GV1196.D52 M83 2000
796.812'092— dc21
[B]
                                                                00-021867

Contents

1 DOWN ON HIS LUCK

"**D**iamond" Dallas Page never thought he would have to confront the question, "How low can a man sink?" Nevertheless, here he was, trying to figure out exactly what he had left in his life. He was astounded by his poverty. Only recently he had been worth $6.6 million. Now it was all gone. His girlfriend, the beautiful Kimberly, had left him for his archrival, Johnny B. Badd. He was jobless and his wrestling career was gone.

Page did not believe he could sink any further than he found himself in the early months of 1996. Page was in an unusual situation for a man who was so far down on his luck: he could trace the development of every one of the events that placed him in the gutter, and that's what made it all so painful. Living on the streets is one thing, but having the clarity of memory and sharpness of intelligence to know exactly how you put yourself there is something else.

The evening of September 17, 1995, was a night that held enormous promise for Page—the World Championship Wrestling (WCW) Fall Brawl pay-per-view event. Thousands of screaming fans had packed the Asheville, North Carolina, Civic Center. They weren't screaming for Page, however. They were screaming against him as he stepped into the ring to

---

In 1996, Page found himself at the bottom of the ladder again. But even though he had lost his girlfriend, his money, and his WCW title, he managed to retain his pride.

face the Renegade, the WCW television champion. Eight minutes and seven seconds later, they were booing loudly when Max Muscle, Page's nefarious sidekick at the time, held the Renegade's legs, allowing Page to score the pin.

Page was WCW TV champion, and it was a night to remember. He had finally captured his first major title. It was an impressive showing for someone who started out as a manager, became a television commentator, and relatively late in the game, decided that he'd rather make his living inside the ring than out of it.

Page's archrival Johnny B. Badd, known today as Marc Mero, took Kimberly and the WCW TV title away from DDP in early 1996.

Page was convinced there wasn't a man in the world who could beat him. He was wrong. At WCW's Halloween Havoc pay-per-view event on October 29, Page put his newly won WCW TV title on the line against Johnny B. Badd and lost it.

Page wrestled his heart out, but Badd was the better man that night, at least inside the ring. Unfortunately for Page, at around the time of that pay-per-view event, Kimberly was starting to realize that Badd might be the better man outside the ring as well.

"I'm tired of being treated like a possession," she said, and rightfully so. She was fed up with Page pushing her around. One of the most beautiful women to grace a wrestling ring, she was a competitor in the Miss U.S.A. fitness competition. Yet Page treated her with no respect. She thought that with Badd, maybe it would be different.

Of course, seeing Kimberly with another man enraged Page. He couldn't believe this was happening to him. His jealousy intensified to the point where he could hardly think straight. At WCW's World War III event on November 26, 1995, Badd pinned Page again. In a subsequent rematch, Kimberly did the seemingly unthinkable: she helped Badd beat Page. During the match, she threw a chain into the ring, and Badd used it to beat up Page.

Page was infuriated. Kimberly was speaking out on television, saying how much she liked Johnny B. Badd and talking about how Page had mistreated her. For Page, it was a matter of humiliation stacked on top of humiliation.

Then Page made another mistake: at WCW's SuperBrawl VI pay-per-view card on February

11, 1996, he agreed to put up every penny he owned—$6.6 million—if Badd would agree to return Kimberly to him if he won. It was an absurd agreement, but Page was blinded by jealousy.

The match ended with Page staring at the ceiling, his money gone. He could no longer afford the services of Max Muscle. He had to sell a pair of his wrestling tights at a WCW TV taping to raise money to pay his bills.

A few weeks later, Page's fortunes appeared to finally take a turn for the better. Badd lost the WCW TV title to Lex Luger on February 17, 1996, and shortly afterward departed from the federation, leaving Kimberly behind. Earlier in

Kimberly, left, "Diamond" Dallas Page's partner, dances with the Nitro Girls, a dance squad she organized for WCW.

the year, Page and Badd had agreed to wrestle a loser-leaves-WCW match at the Uncensored pay-per-view on March 10, 1996. With Badd gone, who would Page wrestle? Would the retirement stipulation still be in effect? Could Page count on help from Kimberly?

The answers were not to Page's liking. His opponent turned out to be the Booty Man, the wrestler formerly known as Brutus Beefcake. The retirement stipulation was still in effect. As for Kimberly: she was on the Booty Man's side.

The Booty Man needed 16 minutes to get the job done, and he left the ring with Kimberly clutching his arm. Page had lost Kimberly to yet another man.

Now Page was about to find out exactly how low a man could sink. Kimberly became the Booty Babe to the Booty Man and shunned all of Page's advances. Forced into retirement and penniless because Kimberly had gotten all of his money, Page lived on the streets and begged for work. He accepted an offer to work at the offices of *Pro Wrestling Illustrated* magazine, but didn't even last a day before walking out.

Down on his luck and needing a miracle, Page kept searching and hoping for that one-in-a-million break that would change his fortunes and get him back on track.

Throughout Dallas Page's life, the cards had always fallen right for him. He had faced adversity, but he had always overcome it. He tried to convince himself that he would bounce back— and bounce back strong, even if he had to make fundamental changes in himself.

The world had not heard the last of "Diamond" Dallas Page. He would make sure of that.

2

THE DIAMOND EXCHANGE

"Diamond" Dallas Page was born Page Falkinburg on April 5, 1949, son to Sylvia Falkinburg, who had three children by the time she was 20. Years later, Page would say he was "born wild." Page was the oldest of the children. A brother, Rory, and a sister, Sally, came later. Page did not have the advantage of loving, doting parents who tended to his every need. For the first 21 years of his life, most of the breaks went against him. Both Sylvia and Page S. Falkinburg, Page's father, drank too much. By the time Page was three, his parents had split up. Rory and Sally went to live with their mother, while Page went to live with his father. This was the late 1950s, a time when divorce was still rare and families generally stayed together. So even early in his life, as a result of his parents' divorce, Page was marked as an unusual person.

Despite his father's drinking problems, Page junior had a close relationship with Page senior, and the two enjoyed watching football together. They lived in New Jersey, home of the New York Giants, and Page's father hated the Dallas Cowboys. Perhaps, in his first bit of rebellion, Page loved the Cowboys—and that's how he got the nickname, Dallas, that would stay with him for the rest of his life.

Growing up in the 1950s, Page Falkinburg loved the Dallas Cowboys—his father's least favorite team—and earned himself the nickname "Dallas."

13

When Page was eight, his father left home, and he did not see him again for 10 years. Dallas went to live with his grandmother, Doris Seigel, who was able to instill some discipline and stability in Page's young life. At that point, things took a turn for the better. Grandma Doris provided a good, stable, supportive home. As Page got a little older, sports started playing a big role in his life. He also started watching pro wrestling. While the mat sport fascinated him, it was youth football and hockey that occupied most of Page's free time. His grandmother took him to his games, although she rarely stayed to watch.

At age 12, Page suffered another setback that could have had a lasting negative impact on his life: he was hit by a car and suffered a shattered knee. Doctors told him he could no longer play organized contact sports. There was no way he'd be able to get approval to play football or hockey, so Page went looking for another pastime, another way to satisfy his athletic urges. He was tall for his age (he would grow up to be 6' 5"), and despite the knee injury, he could play basketball.

In eighth grade, he made the St. Peters basketball team in his hometown of Point Pleasant, New Jersey. Page didn't play very much, but he refused to get discouraged. The next year, he made the St. Joseph's High School team, and saw his playing time increase. His hard work was paying off. In 10th grade, he made the varsity team.

Basketball and socializing kept Page in school. He wasn't a good student, and classwork generally bored him. Once he was expelled because of an incident with a couple of his basketball buddies. At the age of 17, while still attending high school, he took his first job at a local bar. His job was mopping floors and stocking crates of beer. Because of his size, he was soon promoted to bouncer.

Page loved the bar business. The crowds, the people, and the lively atmosphere all appealed to him. For the first time in his life, Page started to think that maybe this was what he wanted to do for a living.

When fast-talking manager Paul E. Dangerously left the AWA, Dallas Page was hired to fill his shoes.

After finishing high school, Page attended Ocean County College in New Jersey, where he continued to play basketball, once scoring 30 points in a game. After two years at Ocean County, he accepted a full athletic scholarship to Coastal Carolina University in South Carolina.

Page hated being away at school. He got sick and lost 20 pounds. After only six weeks, he decided to go back home to New Jersey, where there were two options on his mind: getting into the bar business and getting into pro wrestling.

"I learn from a mistake," Page told *The Wrestler* magazine. "I don't look at it as a negative. I look at as, 'Cool, I know how to get around that.' I think more than anything, if a person's negative, they're going to be negative unless they get around a person like me, who will make them positive. People like me who have bounced around their whole lives have an advantage over people who don't, because I can adapt to any situation."

By age 21, Page was hanging around a lot of bars, and, in his spare time, learning some wrestling moves from a pro wrestler named Tito Torres. Before long, Torres got Page a few local matches, and Page realized he liked being in the ring. After just seven matches, though, Page reinjured his knee. His dream of becoming a pro wrestler appeared to be over before it had really begun.

So Page turned back to what he knew best. He got a chance to run his own bar in New Jersey. The nightlife was great, he always had a woman on his arm, and he was surrounded by famous people and rock stars. Page was a big man at his nightclub, and he never wanted for attention. Yet he couldn't get wrestling off of his mind.

In 1988 Page realized there was another side of the sport, a side in which he could take full advantage of his vivacious personality and knack for carrying on a conversation. Wrestling had wrestlers, but it also had talkers and managers.

Page sprung into action. He made a tape of himself and sent it to the American Wrestling Association (AWA), a now defunct but former major federation that operated out of Minneapolis. His timing was fortunate. The AWA had just lost Paul E. Dangerously, a loud, fast-talking, charismatic manager who defected to the National Wrestling Alliance (NWA). The federation needed someone to replace him.

Page was summoned to Las Vegas for an interview. The AWA wasted no time hiring him as the manager of Badd Company, the tag team of Paul Diamond and Pat Tanaka. Page Falkinburg left his old name and life behind. From now on, he would be "Diamond" Dallas Page (DDP). He had realized his goal of getting involved in pro wrestling by making his own opportunities. Now he would try to make some more.

3

A DIFFERENT APPROACH

The bright lights of Las Vegas provided the perfect spotlight for "Diamond" Dallas Page to start his wrestling career. Glitz, glamour, beautiful women, and lots of excitement—all the things he loved about working in a nightclub—were at his fingertips in Vegas.

By the late 1980s, the AWA was well past its glory years and was considered a sick cousin to more powerful wrestling organizations like the World Wrestling Federation (WWF) and the NWA. However, it wasn't a bad place for a man to get his start in the ring. Some talented stars moved through AWA rings in those years, including Shawn Michaels, the Road Warriors, Curt Hennig, Scott Hall, Jerry Lawler, and Larry Zbyszko—all of whom went on to enjoy success in other federations. Badd Company proved to be the perfect tag team for Page.

Soon after Page was hired by the AWA, he stepped into a high-pressure situation: a match between Badd Company and AWA World tag team champions the Midnight Rockers on March 19, 1988, in Las Vegas. The Rockers, a talented, high-flying tag team, had held the belts since December 27, 1987, and were extremely popular with AWA fans. The Rockers later became Marty Jannetty and Shawn Michaels, the former WWF World heavyweight champion.

Page enjoyed success as a manager in the AWA, NWA, and WCW, handling Badd Company and the Freebirds, as well as Bam Bam Bigelow, Johnny Ace, Dick Slater, Scott Hall, and Colonel DeBeers.

Dallas Page led his team, Badd Company, to a 1988 victory over Midnight Rockers Marty Jannetty and Shawn Michaels, left, who had to surrender their AWA championship belts.

Page passed his first big managerial test in a way that impressed wrestling fans not only in the AWA, but throughout the wrestling world. Paul Diamond and Pat Tanaka, motivated by the infusion of excitement that their new manager provided, stunned the Rockers and managed to capture their first AWA World tag team championship.

Page was never shy about interfering in Badd Company's matches. In fact, he wasn't shy about anything. As for his scruples, the fans quickly found out about those when Page started managing the notorious Colonel DeBeers, the racist South African whose political views hardly belonged in a wrestling ring.

Politics aside, however, Page's leadership made Badd Company a winning team. They held the belts for nearly a year before losing to Ken Patera and Brad Rheingans on March 25, 1989.

Unfortunately for Page, the AWA was on a downward spiral. Attendance was way down, and television ratings were miserable. Although Page was with the AWA for a year, he actually worked only 12 dates, because the federation filmed several TV shows in one day. The AWA's demise was inevitable in an era when the WWF and WCW were quickly transforming and super-charging the sport; it folded in 1991, well after Page had left the federation.

After leaving the sinking AWA, Page relied on his talking skills to land him his next job as a color commentator for Florida Championship Wrestling (FCW). Page worked alongside the legendary TV wrestling announcer Gordon Solie, known as "the Walter Cronkite of professional wrestling." Page also managed Johnny Ace, Dick Slater, and Bam Bam Bigelow. In 1990, Page received a tryout with the WWF as a TV commentator, but he didn't get the job.

Page hadn't left his past life behind and was still working in the nightclub business when Florida Championship Wrestling folded in 1991. He was about to leave the nightclubs behind. In early 1991, Page signed his first managerial contract with the NWA, soon to be transformed into WCW.

Something else happened to Page in 1991—he married Kimberly, the woman he had met in 1989. Kimberly and Page were different in almost every way. He grew up bouncing from home to home and working in nightclubs. She had a master's degree in advertising and was a fitness fanatic. He was wild. She was his stabilizing force.

"I wouldn't have squat if it wasn't for her, because I'm just a rambling man," Page said years later. "She talked me into having a house. I'd have five Harleys and live in an apartment if it was up to me."

Good fortune in Page's private life coincided with good fortune in his professional life. Page got his first major break when he became manager of the legendary Freebirds, the tag team of Jim Garvin and Michael Hayes. Hayes and Garvin, who both had long rock-star hair and wore dark sunglasses, were as flamboyant as Page. On February 24, at Wrestle War '91, the Freebirds defeated Doom—Ron Simmons and Butch Reed—for the NWA World tag team championship.

The victory was partially engineered by Page. Before the match, he introduced the team's new road manager, Big Daddy Dink, who was also known as the legendary Sir Oliver Humperdink. Page left ringside when the match started, but Dink stuck around and interfered in the match, leading to the Freebirds's victory. In his first two managerial stints, Page had helped his charges win the AWA World tag team championship and the NWA World tag team championship, a dual accomplishment that few managers have achieved in their entire careers.

The Freebirds lost the belts a few weeks later, just before the largest member of the

Dallas Page shocked fans when he agreed to manage Colonel DeBeers, the racist South African wrestler.

NWA, Jim Crockett Promotions, was renamed WCW. At about that time, Page added another wrestler to his stable: Scott Hall, who used the name "the Diamond Studd."

The Freebirds scored their next big victory when they upset the Young Pistols for the vacant WCW U.S. tag team title. Of course, their victory was controversial and featured interference by not only Big Daddy Dink, but also by the new masked Freebird, Fantasia.

"Who is Fantasia?" Page said. "That's for me to know and for WCW to find out. Now with the Freebirds champions again and Fantasia and the Diamond Studd in my stable, I'm gonna be the most powerful manager in WCW."

He certainly had an unusual cast of characters. Take Diamond Studd, for instance. His feud with Tom Zenk started because Studd wanted to be "the biggest stud in WCW." Studd and Page combined in a heinous attack on

Among the many wrestlers who joined Page's "Diamond mine" stable of wrestlers in the early 1990s was the Diamond Studd, known today as Scott Hall.

Zenk, making onlookers wonder whether Studd and Page were jealous of the Z-Man's good looks. Page and Studd denied it. At the 1991 Great American Bash, Studd prevailed, thanks to DDP's interference. The Freebirds also continued to benefit from Page's interference, until losing the belts to the Patriots in late August.

Meanwhile, Page was getting a bit of an itch that was only partially satisfied by his part-time work as a color commentator in the WCW broadcast booth. He wanted to wrestle. On the advice of former wrestler Magnum T.A., Page headed to the Power Plant, a wrestling school in Atlanta. There, Jake Roberts, the Assassin, and wrestling legend Dusty Rhodes transformed Page into a wrestler.

"I knew I had all the potential in the world to be a top guy," Page told *Pro Wrestling Illustrated*. "Scott Hall told me, 'It's going to take you 10 years.' I said, 'It'll take me half that.'"

The power of positive thinking had carried him this far. He hoped it could carry him a little farther.

FROM FAMINE TO FEAST

4

With his usual confidence, but just a little trepidation, "Diamond" Dallas Page stepped into the ring as a wrestler for the first time on November 18, 1991. He had plenty of support in his corner. The Diamond Studd was happy to help out. Although Page and Studd didn't walk away with a victory that night, DDP's debut impressed many watchers, including wrestlers and TV announcers.

Being a wrestler instead of a manager didn't mean Page was going to keep his mouth shut. On the contrary, after Page was pinned by new archrival Johnny B. Badd in Chattanooga, Tennessee, Page challenged Badd to wrestle Paul Lee. Page told Badd that if he won, he'd give him $500. When Badd pinned Lee, he had to forcibly take the money from Page.

Page's next test was against P.N. News, a 401-pound brawler whose "broken record" splash was a devastating finishing maneuver. To nobody's surprise, P.N. News needed only three-and-a-half minutes to win the match with his splash. Page got up and walked to the locker room a lot slower than he had walked to the ring.

Despite a pretty good start, Page wasn't yet dazzling anybody with his wrestling ability. He did continue to impress with his managerial skills, bringing in WCW stars like Scotty

---

In 1991 Page made the difficult transition from manager to professional wrestler and constantly dreamed up new ways to promote himself in the ring.

Flamingo—who would later be known as Raven—and Vinnie Vegas—who would later be known as Diesel and, after that, by his real name of Kevin Nash. Page and Vegas occasionally teamed, but they were no match for experienced former world tag team champions like Rick and Scott Steiner.

The losses piled up for DDP. Van Hammer beat him numerous times. Vegas and Page couldn't even beat lesser tag team competition,

Vinnie Vegas, a.k.a. Kevin Nash, was friends with Dallas Page, and the two occasionally teamed up in WCW.

such as Ron Simmons and Junkyard Dog. A series of matches with Johnny B. Badd might have vaulted DDP into WCW's top 10, if he had won. He didn't. Badd, a former Golden Glove boxing champion, had a lethal knockout punch, and he used it time and again against Page. DDP didn't crack the top 10, and he suffered further indignity when, in two consecutive pay-per-view events, he wrestled in the "dark match," the warm-up bout held prior to the actual pay-per-view card. Page's spotlight was getting dimmer by the day.

What Page was suffering through wasn't unusual. After all, he had only been wrestling for a few months. Most wrestlers get some experience in the small, independent federations before trying their hands at the big time. Because Page was already in WCW as a manager, he decided to stay in WCW as a wrestler. An analysis of Page that appeared in the September 7, 1992, issue of the *Pro Wrestling Illustrated Weekly* newsletter told the story of his rookie year. "Though Page is determined to make the switch from manager to wrestler," it said, "he still has quite a way to go before he moves into championship contention. He tries to make up for that with a toughness fueled by arrogance."

That arrogance was on display at Clash of the Champions XXI on November 18, 1992, in Macon, Georgia. Scotty Flamingo, who claimed that he, not Badd, was the "prettiest man in WCW" (a catchphrase of Badd's), had made the serious mistake of challenging Badd to a boxing match. There really was no way Flamingo could beat the former boxer, unless he cheated, which is what he did.

DDP was Flamingo's corner man for the match, and between rounds, he filled Flamingo's right glove with water. That enabled Flamingo to score a stunning—and totally illegal—knockout.

Fate, however, was not on Page's side. In early 1993, Page tore the rotator cuff in his shoulder during a tag team match against Tex Slazenger and Shanghai Pierce, and was side-lined for 11 months. As a kid, a knee injury had prevented him from playing football and hockey. At age 21, when he was thinking of becoming a pro wrestler, another knee injury had stalled his career. And now, just when he had finally decided what he wanted to do with his life, a bum shoulder threatened to foil his plans.

But positive thinking had always been the theme of Page's life, and he wasn't going to let an injury get him down. After undergoing surgery to repair his shoulder, Page used his free time wisely. He watched tapes of matches and studied opponents. Veteran wrestler Jake "the Snake" Roberts taught him the psycholog-ical aspects of wrestling. When he was ready to wrestle again, Page went back into training. Finally, in early 1994, he made his return to the ring, but Page wrestled infrequently and beat only the bottom-of-the-barrel wrestlers, the ones nobody had ever heard of and would never hear of again. Frustrated by WCW's refusal to match him against top wrestlers, Page came up with a gimmick in which he'd pick a name out of a fishbowl and challenge that person to a match. Often, the challenge was refused.

Page continued to look for ways to promote himself. He hired a bodyguard, Max Muscle. He was escorted to the ring by a bevy of beautiful women he called Diamond Dolls. One of those Diamond Dolls was his wife, Kimberly. Page had no shortage of gimmicks. Kimberly became his only Diamond Doll, and her primary job— besides looking good and attending to Page's every need—was rating DDP's moves in the ring. She'd hold up a number, from 1 to 10, depending upon how impressive the move was. But she wasn't allowed to judge for herself. Page would loudly order her to hold up the card with "10" or the card with "10+" on it.

Hoping to advance his own wrestling career, Dallas Page sought advice from Jake "the Snake" Roberts, who helped him master the art of psyching out his opponents.

In one of the lowest points of his career, Page lost a loser-leaves-the-federation match to the Booty Man, a.k.a. Brutus "the Barber" Beef-cake in 1996.

That got Page a little bit of attention, although most of the attention was directed toward the beautiful Kimberly. Meanwhile, the losses continued piling up. Then Page came up with a new gimmick, challenging wrestlers to armwrestling matches and offering a prize most of them couldn't refuse—a date with Kimberly.

Page scored one victory after another, although his opponents usually weren't very impressive. Then along came Dave Sullivan, a goofy wrestler who carried a live rabbit with him to the ring. Page challenged Sullivan to a match at the 1995 Great American Bash. If Page won, he'd get the rabbit. If Sullivan won, he'd get a date with Kimberly. Sullivan won and got the date, but he was attacked after the match by Page and Max Muscle.

Page was enraged when Sullivan actually went on the date with Kimberly, and Kimberly was pleasantly surprised when Sullivan treated her with respect. After all, Page hadn't treated her with much respect. Page got a measure of revenge when he defeated Sullivan at Bash at the Beach on July 16, 1995, ending the feud and starting a new chapter in his career. He actually started to win.

At Clash of the Champions XXI on August 6, 1995, Kimberly was in Page's corner when he defeated Alex Wright, a talented wrestler from Germany. For the first time in his career, Page cracked the WCW top 10 ratings. Then, with the help of Max Muscle, Page won his first title when he beat WCW TV champion the Renegade at Fall Brawl '95 in September.

Thanks to Max's interference, Page kept piling up the wins in title defenses. His signature finishing move, the "diamond cutter," had actually become one of wrestling's most effective maneuvers. Perhaps, however, Page made the mistake of thinking himself unbeatable; at the next pay-per-view event, he lost the TV title to his former nemesis, Johnny B. Badd. He also lost Kimberly, who had agreed to join Badd if Page lost.

Page was beside himself with anger, especially when he saw how much Kimberly enjoyed being with Badd. His anger didn't help him. Badd easily defended the title at World War III, and even got Kimberly's help to beat Page in another rematch.

Page's fortunes went from bad to worse. He lost every cent he owned to Kimberly when he lost to Badd at SuperBrawl '96. He thought things had taken a turn for the better when Badd lost the TV title to Lex Luger and left the federation and Kimberly behind.

Then Page wrestled the Booty Man in a loser-leaves-the-federation match at Uncensored '96. Page lost in the worst possible way when Kimberly slapped him across the face and the Booty Man rolled him up for the pin. The Booty Man left the ring with Kimberly, who started calling herself the Booty Babe.

Page was destitute, but optimism remained his greatest asset. It saved him again. Refusing to give up and admit defeat, Page searched for a loophole in his contract with the Booty Man. Originally, Page was scheduled to wrestle Badd in a loser-leaves-the-federation match at Uncensored. When Badd lost to Luger and departed from WCW, Page had agreed to wrestle the Booty Man. Two months after the Uncensored match, WCW lawyers ruled that the retirement stipulation was not in effect due to the replacement opponent.

Upbeat and ready to take advantage of his second chance, Page returned to the ring in early May. With his return, Page entered himself in the Lethal Lottery at WCW's Slamboree '96 pay-per-view in May. The format of the Lethal Lottery is highly unusual. Tag team pairings are chosen by a blind draw, meaning enemies could end up teaming with enemies, and friends could end up fighting friends. Page was teamed with the Barbarian, who was neither friend nor foe. They won their first- and second-round matches.

That earned them a spot in the eight-man Battlebowl battle royal, which was every man for himself. The prize was WCW's Lord of the Ring title. Page appeared to have been eliminated from Battlebowl when he was thrown over the top rope and onto the arena floor, but no referee saw it happen, so Page climbed back into the ring, used his "diamond cutter" to pin Bobby Eaton, Johnny Grunge, and the Barbarian, and won the match.

DDP was WCW's Lord of the Ring. "I'm in the perfect situation," Page boasted. "I'm on top of the world." He was ready to stay there for a good long time.

5

HERO OF THE PEOPLE

The words were ringing in "Diamond" Dallas Page's ears: "It's going to take you 10 years," Scott Hall had warned him when Page first went to wrestling school. Ten years to make it big in the ring. Page also clearly remembered his own response: "It'll take me half that." That was in 1991. Five years had passed since Page had stepped into the ring as a wrestler for the first time.

Page defeated Marcus Bagwell at the June 1996 Great American Bash, and veteran star Hacksaw Duggan at Bash at the Beach a month later. Page feuded briefly with Eddy Guerrero, a talented mat and aerial wrestler, and lost to him at Clash of the Champions XXXIII, but used three diamond cutters to injure and sideline Guerrero. Chavo Guerrero took his uncle's place at Fall Brawl, lost to Page, and was also injured by the diamond cutter. When Eddy Guerrero returned to the ring, Page pinned him cleanly at Halloween Havoc '96.

But much bigger things were happening in wrestling. Kevin Nash and Scott Hall—Page's former Diamond Studd— had returned to WCW from the WWF. At first, they called themselves the Outsiders, but when Hulk Hogan, one of the most popular wrestlers in history, shocked the world and joined the group, they became the New World Order (NWO).

"Diamond" Dallas Page, bottom, hoists Curt Hennig during their match at Starrcade '97. Page used his diamond cutter finishing move to defeat Hennig for his first WCW U.S. title.

When the NWO started recruiting new members, Page complained that Nash and Hall, his former friends, should have asked him to join the group when it was formed. Perhaps because he was insulted, and perhaps because he simply had a change of heart, Page turned down Hall and Nash when they finally did ask him to join.

In late 1996, the NWO was the most hated group in wrestling. Their cheating tactics, sneak attacks, and the simple joy they got out of injuring opponents made them enemies of the fans. Their attack on WCW—their goal was to take over the federation—was unprecedented in the sport's history. WCW needed defending, and it needed heroes. DDP took his first step toward becoming a hero when he used his diamond cutter on Hall. It was his way of saying, "Thanks, but no thanks."

One of the highlights of Starrcade on December 29, 1996, was the final round of the tournament for the vacant WCW U.S. title. Page won his way into the finals where his opponent was Eddy Guerrero. Page might have had a chance on his wrestling ability alone, but he had no chance when Hall, Nash, and Syxx (later known as X-Pac in the WWF) attacked him during the match. Guerrero won the match and the U.S. title, but he was also attacked by the NWO.

Page's war with the NWO heated up. He used his diamond cutter to pin Syxx a week after Starrcade. At Clash of the Champions XXXIV on January 22, 1997, Page helped Guerrero in his match against Scott Norton, a member of the NWO. Page interfered and used a diamond cutter on Norton, enabling Guerrero to score the pin.

Four days later, the wrestling world focused its attention on Souled Out, the first NWO-sponsored pay-per-view event. Page was in the middle of his match with Norton when several members of the NWO, including Nash and Hall, walked to ringside and offered Page an NWO T-shirt. If he took it and put it on, he'd be a member of the NWO. If he didn't, he'd remain on the side of WCW. Page took the T-shirt, pulled it over his head and onto his body. Then he used a diamond cutter on Norton, walked away from the ring, and tore off the T-shirt. At WCW's *Nitro* broadcast on February 24, 1997, Hall challenged Page to a match. Page accepted, and they wrestled later in the night. During the match, new NWO member Randy Savage and several other NWO members attacked Page, dropped him with a series of elbowsmashes, and covered him with spray paint. Page had become the NWO's enemy, tops on the hit list of the most dangerous group in wrestling. Simply because he had said no to the NWO, DDP was suddenly becoming one of the hottest stars in the sport.

Around this time, Page and Kimberly started discussing whether she was ready to rejoin him in the ring. "We're just getting some stuff straightened out, discussing a few things that I am not at liberty to talk to you about at the moment," Page told *Pro Wrestling Illustrated Weekly*.

Actually, there were two things they were talking about: one, whether Kimberly, if she returned to the ring, should reveal that she and DDP were married. And two, whether she should accept an offer from a popular men's magazine to pose for its celebrities issue. Their answer to both questions was yes.

When NWO member Randy Savage attacked Page's wife Kimberly, DDP began a one-man feud against Savage and the NWO that was so red-hot, it was voted feud of the year in 1997.

Kimberly made her return at Uncensored '97 on March 16. She was in the locker room area while Page was being interviewed by WCW announcer Gene Okerlund about Randy Savage, who had just joined the NWO.

"Savage refuses to acknowledge me," Page complained. "Macho, if you're that much of a Savage, snap into this!" Page thought Savage wasn't anywhere near Charleston, South Carolina, that night. He was wrong.

Savage and his manager, Elizabeth, came walking out smiling and laughing. Page didn't know why. He had no idea. Then Savage pulled out a copy of the magazine that featured Kimberly. What happened next angered Page even more: Kimberly came stumbling out from the dressing room covered with spray paint, the result of Savage and Elizabeth trying to humiliate her. When Page tried to defend his beautiful wife, he was attacked by Savage and spray-painted, too.

Ironically, his wife's humiliation had become Page's fast route to fame. Savage vs. Page was the main event of the Spring Stampede pay-per-view on April 6, 1997, and a sellout crowd showed up at the Convention Center in Tupelo, Mississippi, to watch these new rivals go at it in a brutal no-disqualification match.

Page and Savage battled out of the ring, onto the ring apron, and into the crowd. The bitter energy of Page's assault was matched only by Savage's manic fury. When the action returned to the ring, Page tried to use his diamond cutter on Savage, but Savage countered. Then Savage went nuts. He attacked the ring announcer, slammed a chair over Page's back, and beat up the referee. When a substitute referee took over, Page scored with his diamond cutter, then covered Savage for the pin. But Savage wasn't done yet. He grabbed Kimberly by the hair and probably would have hit her had NWO head Eric Bischoff not warned him.

Wrestling's hottest war continued with more victories for Page, but Savage's attacks on Kimberly had already done their damage. Page started to wonder whether it was a good idea to have his wife around a wrestling ring. Before, Kimberly was simply Page's Diamond Doll, his valet, his escort to the ring. It was different now that people knew they were married, and Page was having a hard time focusing on his matches when she was around. He always had to worry about her getting attacked.

"The NWO guys knows that they can get under my skin by threatening her," Page said. "I want her here, but I have to be smart about the situation."

The NWO continued its all-out attack on Page. He had become their main enemy. Page was leading WCW's charge against the NWO, fighting what seemed like a one-man battle against these nefarious outsiders. He attacked Savage at Slamboree '97; Hogan and Savage returned the favor at the next *Nitro*, injuring Page's ribs.

Their next big showdown came at the 1997 Great American Bash in a lights-out, no-disqualification match. Savage was out of control that night. He beat up two referees and a photographer, then he beat up Page. DDP was on the verge of defeat when Savage went to the top rope for his elbowdrop, but Page got up, grabbed Savage, and connected with a diamond cutter. He was about to score the pin when Scott Hall interfered. Savage got up and struck Page with Hall's WCW World tag team title belt, then Hall floored Page, setting up the pin for Savage.

Enraged by Hall's interference, Page challenged Savage and Hall to a tag team match at Bash at the Beach. Page had a mystery partner, who turned out to be former AWA World heavyweight champion Curt Hennig. Hennig, however, couldn't be trusted. He walked out on Page during the match, leaving Page in an impossible situation. Hall and Savage won the match.

Page then enlisted the help of Lex Luger for a tag team match against Hall and Nash. Page and Luger won the match, but only by disqualification after they were attacked by the rest of the NWO. The fact was, the NWO really didn't care whether it won or lost its matches. It only cared about attacking and injuring its enemies.

At Clash of the Champions XXXV on August 21, 1997, Savage was allowed to substitute for Nash and joined Hall in a world tag team title defense against Luger and Page. Again, Savage's main concern was hurting Page, and he punched DDP in the right eye, temporarily blinding him. Luger went over to help his partner, but the sightless Page thought he was a member of the NWO and gave Luger a diamond cutter. Hall covered Luger for the pin.

The next week at *Nitro*, Luger accidentally placed Page in his "torture rack" after DDP had come to his aid. And the following week, again

DDP, left, and Sting go after each other in a title match for the WCW Mayhem Championship belt on May 13, 1999, in Los Angeles. In 1997, Page's rival Hulk Hogan put on white face paint and disguised himself as Sting in order to attack and injure Page at Halloween Havoc.

at *Nitro*, Luger accidentally nailed Page with a forearm, leading to a victory for Hall and Savage.

The NWO loved seeing Page and Luger, two of their biggest rivals, having difficulties, and they were ready to witness the breakup of this duo when Page and Luger went head-to-head at *Nitro*. If there was one thing that could keep Page and Luger together, however, it was the NWO. When the NWO interfered, Page and Luger immediately realized who their real enemies were. After dealing with the NWO, they embraced in the ring. At Fall Brawl '97 in September, Page and Luger again beat Savage and Hall.

Savage caused grief for Page even when they weren't wrestling each other. On October 6, 1997, Page got a shot against WCW TV champion Disco Inferno. This was a marvelous opportunity for Page. DDP appeared to have the TV title in his grasp when he stunned Disco

Inferno with the diamond cutter. Inferno was laid out in the center of the ring. Page moved in for the kill, but then Savage interfered. Page's attention immediately turned to the man he hated most. They took their brawl outside the ring. Savage was just about to piledrive Page onto the concrete floor when WCW interim commissioner Roddy Piper stopped him. That gave Page the chance to give Savage the diamond cutter onto the concrete. Savage had to be carted away on a stretcher.

Page and Savage had their next showdown in a sudden death match at Halloween Havoc in Las Vegas. Under the rules, the man who couldn't continue after being knocked out for 10 seconds was the loser. The match was fought all over the arena. Elizabeth attacked Page. Kimberly grabbed Elizabeth by the hair and dragged her away. Page and Savage fought down the runway and to the backstage area of the MGM Grand Garden Arena. When the match returned to the ring, the referee was inadvertently knocked out. Suddenly, a man who looked like Sting—one of the most popular wrestlers in WCW—appeared at ringside. "Sting" nailed Page with a baseball bat, knocking him out cold. Page couldn't respond to the 10-count. Savage was the winner.

The imposter Sting was NWO member Hulk Hogan, Page's rival. They wrestled at *Nitro*, and Page won by disqualification when the NWO interfered. Hogan got his revenge after the 60-man Battle Royal at the World War III pay-per-view by giving DDP three diamond cutters felling him on top of the WCW World title belt.

Page vs. the NWO, and specifically Page vs. Savage, was wrestling's feud of the year, and one of the most vicious wars the sport had ever seen. Page's one-man fight against the NWO was courageous. No NWO member was safe from Page's wrath.

DDP next set his sights on WCW U.S. champion Curt Hennig, the man who had walked out on him earlier in the year. Interference by the NWO saved Hennig in two matches. Then Page got one of the biggest breaks of his life.

Hennig was scheduled to square off against Ric Flair at Starrcade, WCW's most important annual pay-per-view event, on December 28, 1997. Hennig, however, attacked Flair at the *Nitro* broadcast just days before Starrcade, putting Flair out of the match. Page offered to take Flair's place at Starrcade. Hennig accepted the challenge.

Hennig attacked early and punished Page. Page rallied and scored with a slingshot cross-bodyblock that sent Hennig flying into the crowd. When the action returned to the ring, Hennig and Page engaged in a furious battle, exchanging punishment and near-pins. Then Hennig whipped Page into the ropes. Page rebounded, but not into Hennig's waiting arms. He caught Hennig with the diamond cutter. Hennig crashed to the mat. Page went in for the pin and got it. As 1997 came to an end, "Diamond" Dallas Page's first WCW U.S. championship was just beginning.

6

THE CHAMPION

"**D**iamond" Dallas Page was exhausted. He had spent most of 1997 waging a one-man war against the NWO. After so many battles against Randy Savage, Hulk Hogan, Curt Hennig, and the rest of the NWO, Hennig had managed to win WCW's second most important singles belt, the U.S. championship. And after battling so many enemies, he decided to battle a friend.

In early February, Page offered a U.S. title shot to Chris Benoit. Page thought he deserved it. Benoit was a great wrestler who had been loyal to WCW. Of course, loyalty meant nothing to some people, including Raven, who, as Scotty Flamingo, had once been Page's friend. In fact, Page had even recruited Flamingo into WCW. When Page battled Benoit at the February 5, 1998, edition of *Thunder*, Raven's Flock spoiled the show and destroyed the match.

First the NWO, now the Flock. Page never seemed to run out of enemies. And he always seemed to be the lone man against the group. Raven and his Flock attacked Page at *Nitro*. Raven's evil influence had an effect on Benoit, who turned against Page, setting up a three-way match involving Page, Raven, and Benoit at Uncensored '98. Page was in trouble. He was down on the mat and in pain, watching while Benoit tried

---

DDP, right, poses with Booker T of Harlem Heat. Page defeated Booker's other half, Stevie Ray, at the War Games match of Fall Brawl '98 for a shot at WCW champion Bill Goldberg.

"Diamond" Dallas Page, left, battles his old enemy Hulk Hogan during a September 1999 match at Madison Square Garden in New York.

to finish off Raven and win the U.S. title. Somehow, he made it back, executed his diamond cutter on Raven, and scored the pin to retain the belt.

The feud intensified. Page was appearing on the show *MTV Live* when Raven sneak-attacked him from behind and stole the U.S. title belt. For Page, 1998 was turning into a repeat of 1997, only this time Raven and the Flock were his enemies instead of Savage and the NWO.

At Spring Stampede on April 19, 1998, Raven and Page not only fought in the ring, but on the ring apron, down the aisle, and onto a stage.

They used garbage cans, fence posts, and any-thing they could get their hands on—even a kitchen sink. In the end, Page couldn't deal with all of the Flock's interference. It was as if he was fighting a one-against-five battle. Horace Boulder, Hulk Hogan's nephew, bashed Page with a stop sign; a three-count later, DDP's first U.S. title reign was over.

Meanwhile, the wrestling world was under-going another big change. Internal problems had caused the NWO to split into two compet-ing factions: NWO Hollywood, led by Hollywood Hogan and Eric Bischoff, and NWO Wolfpac, led by Kevin Nash. One of the members of the Wolfpac was Savage, who had turned against Hogan earlier in the year. The question being asked of every wrestler in WCW was, "Whose side are you on?" Page's answer was "Neither."

"I've had to fight for every little thing in life I ever got," Page told *The Wrestler* magazine. "That's why joining NWO Hollywood or the Wolfpac never appealed to me. I take pride in relying only on myself to get things done. Everybody should."

He hated NWO Hollywood. Page all but declared war on Hogan, saying he wanted revenge for the things the NWO had done to him over the past year.

At *Thunder* on June 4, Page teamed with Lex Luger against The Giant and Brian Adams. This was big news because Luger was a mem-ber of the Wolfpac. Page won the match with his diamond cutter, and Luger invited him to join the Wolfpac.

Four days later at *Nitro*, the Wolfpac came out and invited Page to the ring so that he could announce his decision. They held a

NWO Wolfpac wanted Page to join them, but DDP preferred to remain an individual and fight his own battles.

red-and-black Wolfpac T-shirt for him to accept or decline. Page came out wearing a DDP T-shirt and was seemingly about to accept the invitation when, out of nowhere, Hogan and National Basketball Association (NBA) star Dennis Rodman of the Chicago Bulls stormed onto the scene, attacked Page, and nailed him with a chair.

Bad feelings died hard. The next week at *Nitro*, Savage revealed that he was against Page joining the Wolfpac, and challenged Page to a match. DDP accepted. "And when I'm done," Page told announcer Gene Okerlund, "I want Hogan and Rodman."

Savage and Page had renewed their rivalry earlier that evening in a match that was officiated by wrestler Roddy Piper. Piper got involved when Savage hit him from behind. Late in the match, Piper rammed both Savage and Page into the steel cage. Members of NWO Hollywood—Bret Hart, Brian Adams, Elizabeth, and others—attacked both men, before Nash made the save.

Rodman's presence in the feud attracted national attention. On June 17, 1998, Rodman and Hogan appeared on *The Tonight Show with Jay Leno*. When Leno told Rodman and Hogan he had a surprise for them, out walked Page with Utah Jazz star Karl Malone. The two sides almost went at it right there. Two days later, WCW held a press conference to announce that Hogan and Rodman would battle Page and Malone at Bash at the Beach. At *Nitro* on June 29, Malone bodyslammed Hogan, then he and Page challenged Rodman to show up the next week.

National media converged on San Diego, California, to watch Hogan and Rodman battle Page and Malone in one of the most hyped matches in wrestling history. Rodman and Hogan dictated the pace of the match, until Malone turned the tide with a series of clotheslines and bodyslams. Page nearly finished off Hogan with a diamond cutter, but Rodman interfered. While Rodman and Malone battled, the Disciple interfered on Hogan's behalf and used his Apocalypse—a version of the diamond cutter—on Page. Then he rolled Hogan on top of Page for the pin.

The next night at *Nitro*, Page was ambushed by NWO Hollywood. On July 20, Page and Bret Hart were named the top contenders for the vacant U.S. title. Page was limping badly because of the attacks by NWO Hollywood, and barely offered a test to Hart, who won the match. Page wasn't mad at Hart, he was mad at Hogan.

"I'm going to get the almighty God of professional wrestling," Page swore, referring to Hogan. Page stomped and cursed. Finally, he challenged Hogan to a match later in the evening. Page won by disqualification in a match that lasted only four minutes before members of NWO Hollywood and the Wolfpac stormed into the ring for an all-out brawl.

NWO Hollywood was not only the most powerful and most evil clique in wrestling, it was the most obnoxious, too. Their latest target was Jay Leno. Eric Bischoff made fun of Leno's famous jutting chin, then started mocking *The Tonight Show*. Hogan declared that Leno would soon have to take a back seat to Bischoff on the late-night talk show scene.

Leno fired back at the hecklers, making fun of Hogan's age and "painted on" beard. Page declared, "Hey, Jay's a class act. Hearing Eric Bischoff and Hollywood Hogan run him down on *Nitro* was a disgrace. If Jay wants to take an active role that bad, then I got his back."

That led to a showdown at Road Wild: Bischoff and Hogan against Page and Leno on August 8 in Sturgis, South Dakota. Page was true to his promise: he put Leno through his paces in the weeks before the match, making sure he was properly trained, and even trained Kevin Eubanks, Leno's bandleader. Leno was impressive. When he hit Bischoff with a low blow, Eubanks bounded into the ring and used a diamond cutter. Leno pinned Bischoff, and WCW World champion Bill Goldberg made sure Hogan and Bischoff didn't get in the last shot.

The next big event for Page and WCW was the War Games match at Fall Brawl '98. In War Games, wrestlers enter the ring one at a time.

The winner—and the recipient of a shot at the WCW World heavyweight title at Halloween Havoc—would be the last man standing.

The match started with Page and Bret Hart going head-to-head for five minutes. Stevie Ray entered next, followed by Sting, Roddy Piper, Lex Luger, Kevin Nash, Hogan, and the Disciple. Although he was the first man in the ring, Page survived and pinned Stevie Ray to win War Games and earn the title shot.

Page vs. Goldberg at Halloween Havoc was one of the best matches of 1998. Goldberg floored Page with collar-and-elbow lockups, then used a series of takedowns and submission holds. Page bravely fought back and used his diamond cutter to hurt Goldberg. Finally, however, Goldberg won the match with a spear and a jackhammer. When the match ended, Goldberg and Page embraced.

Page wasn't ruined by his loss to Goldberg. The next night at *Nitro*, Page defeated Bret Hart to win his second WCW U.S. title. When Hart attacked Page with a chair after the match, Goldberg flew to DDP's rescue. Another feud had started.

This war was even hotter than Page's previous two with Savage and Raven. After losing to Page at World War III, Hart went on a rampage, going after Chris Benoit, Konnan, and Dean Malenko. Hart was a madman. He gleefully used steel chairs on his enemies. Then, on November 30, The Giant interfered on Hart's behalf in a match against Page, and helped him regain the U.S. title. At *Nitro* a week later, Hart challenged Page to a match, but it was merely a setup that enabled The Giant to choke-slam Page through a wooden platform.

During a June 17, 1998, episode of The Tonight Show with Jay Leno, Diamond Dallas Page and Karl Malone challenged Hulk Hogan and Dennis Rodman to a match.

"People like Bret Hart make me want to vomit," Page said in an interview with *The Wrestler* magazine. "He had me convinced for a while there that he had a little pride left. He showed me some guts. I didn't mind him using all the dirty tactics he's ever learned, as long as it was just him against me. The man has turned into an animal. It's sad when he needs The Giant's help to win."

Because of Page's raging popularity, Hart was suddenly the most hated man in WCW. Not that Hart cared.

"Am I making him a little uncomfortable?" Hart asked *The Wrestler*. "I don't control The

Giant. He hates Page as much as I do. He called me an animal? I take that as a compliment. I'm like a seething Canadian wolf ready to rip into his throat."

Page got revenge against The Giant when he used his diamond cutter to win at Starrcade '98, but there was nothing he could do to stop something else that happened at Starrcade— the reunion of NWO Hollywood and NWO Wolfpac into one strong NWO.

"You know, I'm sick and tired of all these cliques around here," Page said at the time. "The NWO, the Four Horsemen, the LWO (Latin World Order). Sometimes I think I'm the only one who remembers that wrestling is a one-on-one sport. 1999 is going to be the year DDP wins the world title. If I have to go through the NWO and take Hogan out to do it, then so be it."

He was never lacking for enemies. When Scott Steiner started making insulting remarks about Kimberly, Page targeted him for revenge, too. Steiner kept harassing Kimberly. Page warned him to stay away from her. Steiner remained defiant.

Although Page knew having Kimberly around could only serve as a distraction, he really had no choice. Kimberly had become the most popular member of the Nitro Girls, a team of beautiful women who performed dance routines during *Nitro* broadcasts. Page took on the role of the Nitro Girls' bodyguard to make sure Steiner didn't interfere with their routines.

One night, Steiner and Kimberly were about to get into a car together. Page stopped them and started brawling with Steiner. When Steiner and Kimberly began to drive away, Steiner pushed Kimberly out of the car. It was a shocking incident. Paramedics placed a neck brace on Kimberly and took her to a nearby hospital.

Once again, a wrestling feud had become a personal matter for Page, and this one became more personal when Page and Steiner agreed that if Steiner beat him at SuperBrawl '99, he would get Kimberly for 30 days.

Page dominated the match. This time, he wasn't going to lose Kimberly. He fought like a man possessed. But Steiner was ruthless, and when Buff Bagwell interfered, Steiner was on his way to a shocking victory. Steiner locked on his "Steiner recliner" finisher and DDP passed out from the pain.

The injury kept Page out of action for a month. When he returned to the ring in late March, he was hungry for revenge. Ric Flair, who was the new WCW president, told Page that before he got to Steiner, he'd have to beat Hogan. Furthermore, he'd have to allow Flair to serve as his manager for the bout. Anxious to get to Steiner, Page agreed to Flair's stipulations. During the match, Flair mistakenly nailed Page with a chair and DDP's chance at revenge was delayed.

At Spring Stampede on April 11, 1999, Page, Hulk Hogan, Sting, and Ric Flair were the contestants in a four-way match for Flair's WCW World title. Page went after Hogan early in the match and sent Hogan limping away as the result of a figure-four leglock. Page battled with Sting and Flair. Sting floored Page with a scorpion deathdrop. Flair caught Sting in a figure-four. Then Randy Savage came out of nowhere and attacked Flair and Sting with a top-rope elbowdrop.

Now all three wrestlers were on their backs. The referee started to count. At nine, Page got up, delivered a diamond cutter on Flair, and covered him for the pin.

For the first time in his life, Page was WCW World heavyweight champion. But the way he had taken advantage of Savage's interference raised questions.

"Six months ago, DDP wouldn't have made the pin, but fair play never got me anywhere, so I took advantage of the situation," Page said. "Let those two hotheads fight it out, Jack. I got the belt, and that's all that matters. In case you haven't figured it out, I ain't wearing the white hat no more."

Page's meaning was clear; the fans could no longer count on him to fight WCW's battles. He had become disgusted a few months earlier when many fans went against him in his war with Scott Steiner.

Perhaps becoming a rulebreaker was the right move for Page, because over the next several months, his career really took off. True, he had suddenly become the most hated man in WCW, but his list of accomplishments piled up like never before. Although he lost the WCW World title to Sting on April 26, 1999, he won it back later the same night in a four-way match that also involved Sting, Kevin Nash, and Bill Goldberg. He lost the belt to Nash two weeks later.

He also became a major contender for the WCW World tag team title after forming the Triad with Bam Bam Bigelow and Kanyon. He and Bigelow won the WCW World tag team belts on May 31, then Page and Kanyon won them again on June 13.

Incredibly, Page sided with Savage, who had been his most hated rival. He feuded with

Goldberg. He also feuded with Flair, who paid the price for having his eye on Kimberly.

In early 2000, Page suffered from lower back pain, the result of some ruptured discs in his back, but he assured fans he would continue to wrestle.

As the millennium drew to a close, "Diamond" Dallas Page was no longer loved. In some corners, he was no longer respected. But he was famous. And though he wasn't charitable toward his opponents in the ring, he was certainly a giving person outside the ring. Page formed a chraritable foundation, "Bang It Out for Books," to combat illiteracy and encourage kids to read. Since December 1998, Page has teamed up with rock star Jon Bon Jovi, actor Chazz Palminteri, and the company Scholastic Books for the Reading, Rock, and Rasslin' Extravaganza, a program that encourages children to read.

"I had dyslexia when I was a kid," Page explained to *The Wrestler*. "It took a long time before it was diagnosed, and some teachers just wrote me off as being stupid. It really tore me up inside. I just couldn't understand why I was having so much trouble trying to read, when everyone else in class picked up on it so easily. It wasn't until I was out of school before I realized what I was missing out on and began to read again. I want to reach out and try to help other kids who have similar problems or don't have access to a lot of books."

Page even spent a year working on his own autobiography, a book called *Positively Page: The Diamond Dallas Page Journey*. Self-published through Positive Publications, the book is available online. "Hollywood" Hulk Hogan wrote the forward to the book, which tells the story of Page's life from childhood through his professional wrestling career.

Page's effort to encourage children to read was another example of his positive attitude. This frame of mind has guided Page during his entire career and turned him into a wrestling superstar.

Fans can also be positive that Page's influence on the sport is far from over.

Chronology

1949   Born Page Falkinburg on April 5, 1949

1988   Signs with the AWA and becomes manager of Badd Company; takes on the name "Diamond" Dallas Page; Badd Company wins the AWA World tag team title from the Midnight Rockers

1990   Works as a color commentator alongside the legendary Gordon Solie for FCW; manages Johnny Ace, Dick Slater, and Bam Bam Bigelow in FCW

1991   Signs his first managerial contract with the NWA and manages the Freebirds; marries Kimberly; the Freebirds win the NWA World tag team championship; the Freebirds win the U.S. tag team title; Page attends wrestling school in Atlanta and makes his wrestling debut on November 18 in WCW

1995   Cracks the WCW top 10 ratings with a victory over Alex Wright at Clash of the Champions XXI; wins the WCW TV title at Fall Brawl from the Renegade; loses the WCW TV title to Badd; named Most Improved Wrestler of the year by the readers of *Pro Wrestling Illustrated*

1996   Loses a match to Badd and has to give all of his money to Kimberly; loses a loser-must-retire match to the Booty Man; finds a loophole in the match contract and is allowed to return; wins WCW's Lord of the Ring tournament

1997   A feud with the NWO makes Page one of the most popular men in wrestling; Kimberly rejoins Page at ringside, igniting a year-long feud with Randy Savage and Elizabeth; wins the WCW U.S. title at Starrcade from Curt Hennig on December 28

1998   Loses the WCW U.S. title at Spring Stampede to Raven; teams with NBA star Karl Malone and loses to Hollywood Hogan and Dennis Rodman at Bash at the Beach; teams with talk show host Jay Leno to beat Eric Bischoff and Hogan at Road Wild; wins the WCW U.S. title from Bret Hart; loses the WCW U.S. title to Bret Hart

1999   Wins a four-way match for the WCW World heavyweight title at Spring Stampede; loses the WCW World heavyweight title on April 26 to Sting; regains the title later the same night; loses the WCW World heavyweight title at Slamboree '99 to Kevin Nash; teams with Bam Bam Bigelow to win the WCW World tag team title

Further Reading

"America's Wrestler: Taking a Page from the Dallas Playbook." *The Wrestler Presents True Life Stories* (Summer 1998): 16–25.

Anderson, Steve. "DDP's Ph.D: Earning His Degree in Grappology." *The Wrestler* (March 1997): 66–69.

Hunter, Matt. *Superstars of Men's Pro Wrestling.* Philadelphia: Chelsea House Publishers, 1998.

Rosenbaum, Dave. "Bigelow, DDP, & Goldberg: WCW's Triple Threat?" *The Wrestler* (July 1999): 30–33.

Rosenbaum, Dave. "'Diamond' Dallas Page Strikes Gold: Now He's the Target of the NWO and WCW!" *Inside Wrestling Digest* (Spring 1998): 79–81.

"Stripped of Their Dignity: Can Kimberly & DDP Ever Re-Cover?" *The Wrestler* (August 1997): 42–45.

Website

The Official "Diamond" Dallas Page website: http://www.ddpbang.com

Index

Photo Credits

All Star Sports: p. 50; AP/Wide World Photos: pp. 12, 43, 54; Blackjack Brown: pp. 2, 6, 18, 36, 46, 60; Jeff Eisenberg Sports Photography: pp. 8, 10, 15, 20, 23, 28, 31, 32, 40, 48; Howard Kernats Photography: pp. 24, 26.

JACQUELINE MUDGE is a frequent contributor to sports and entertainment magazines in the United States. Born in Idaho, she became a wrestling fan at age 11 when her father took her to matches. Although she has a degree in journalism, she left the writing arena for several years in the late-1980s to pursue a career in advertising sales. She returned to the profession—and the sport she loves—in 1995. Her previously published volumes on the mat sport include *Randy Savage: The Story of the Wrestler They Call "Macho Man"* and *Bret Hart: The Story of the Wrestler They Call "The Hitman."*